GW00643235

# GCSE Religious Studies

Christianity: Beliefs & Values

Philip Allan Updates, an imprint of Hodder Education, an Hachette UK company, Market Place, Deddington, Oxfordshire OX15 0SE

**Orders**

Bookpoint Ltd, 130 Milton Park, Abingdon, Oxfordshire OX14 4SB
tel: 01235 827720      fax: 01235 400454      e-mail: uk.orders@bookpoint.co.uk

Lines are open 9.00 a.m.–5.00 p.m., Monday to Saturday, with a 24-hour message answering service. You can also order through our website: www.philipallan.co.uk

© Philip Allan Updates 2009
ISBN 978-1-4441-0180-5

First published in 2004 as *Flashrevise Cards*

Impression number   5   4   3   2   1
Year     2014     2013     2012     2011     2010     2009

Printed in Spain

Hachette UK's policy is to use papers that are natural, renewable and recyclable products and made from wood grown in sustainable forests. The logging and manufacturing processes are expected to conform to the environmental regulations of the country of origin.

P01589

# Monotheism

**Q1** What do Christians understand by the Trinity?

**Q2** What does omnipotent mean?

**Q3** What does omniscient mean?

**Q4** What does omnibenevolent mean?

ANSWERS

# the belief that there is only one true God

**A1** although God is one God, he is known through the three persons of the Father, the Son (Jesus) and the Holy Spirit

**A2** all-powerful

**A3** all-knowing

**A4** perfectly good, or all-loving

***examiner's* note** Omnipotence, omniscience and omnibenevolence are the classical attributes of the God of Christianity, Judaism and Islam, and they have important implications for many other topics in this section.

 **ANSWERS**

# Nature of God

**Q1** What is meant by a 'personal' God?

**Q2** What is meant by an 'impersonal' God?

**Q3** What is meant by an 'immanent' God?

**Q4** What is meant by a 'transcendent' God?

ANSWERS

# the way in which God is known to those who believe in him

**A1** a God who can be known personally and intimately to those who worship him

**A2** a God who has no personal qualities, but is a spirit or an idea in the minds of believers

**A3** a God who is part of the world

**A4** a God who is outside and separate from the world

***examiner's* note** These are sophisticated ideas, but they are important in determining whether believers can really know God or only know *about* God.

# Knowing God

**Q1** Why do some Christians prefer the idea of an immanent God?

**Q2** Why do some Christians prefer the idea of a transcendent God?

**Q3** Suggest three ways in which believers may come to know God.

**Q4** How might Christians see God at work through the Holy Spirit?

ANSWERS

## entering into a relationship with God

**A1** they want to have a close, personal relationship with God

**A2** they want God to be completely different from human beings and to be able to intervene supernaturally in the world

**A3** through prayer, religious experience, miracles, the beauty of creation, the love of other Christians

**A4** through inspiration, prophecy, healing, speaking in tongues and other charismatic phenomena

***examiner's* note** Make sure that you can offer good reasons why these examples could be challenged by atheists as well as by some Christians who do not share these experiences of God.

**3** **ANSWERS**

# Coming to believe in God

**Q1** How might families help their members to believe in God?

**Q2** How might churches help people in their belief?

**Q3** Give two other ways in which people may come to believe in God.

**Q4** Why might people convert to another religion?

ANSWERS

## people are not born believing in God, but need to find a reason to do so

A1 by worshipping and praying together; by bringing up children in a home which places God at its centre

A2 by offering teaching to children and adults who want to learn about the faith; by supporting families in practical and spiritual ways; by making services accessible to people of all ages and circumstances

A3 hearing a talk which moves them, the witness of their friends or colleagues, religious television broadcasts, answered prayer, miracles

A4 they may feel their existing religion leaves too many unanswered questions or makes unacceptable demands on their life

***examiner's* note** Try to be very specific in your answers to these questions. You need to be clear that people are not religious because they are told that they should be, but because they have chosen to be.

**4** ANSWERS

# Miracles

**Q1** Name at least two different types of miracle.

**Q2** Name two occasions on which Jesus performed a miracle.

**Q3** Give two reasons why Christians believe that God performs miracles.

**Q4** Give two reasons why atheists and some Christians do not believe in miracles.

ANSWERS

# violation of a law of nature, or beneficial or fortunate interventions by God

**A1** healing of the sick, casting out demons, raising the dead, nature miracles, food multiplication miracles

**A2** raising of Lazarus and of Jairus' daughter; feeding of 5,000; turning water into wine, and many more

**A3** they believe that miracles are a sign of God's love and power; they are a way in which God can make himself known to people today

**A4** there is insufficient evidence; miracles can all be explained non-religiously; if God could perform miracles he would do more of them, or more important ones

***examiner's* note** Some Christians believe that miracles were only for the time of Jesus and his apostles, others that they are a gift from God to believers for all time.

 **ANSWERS**

# Religious experience

**Q1** Give an example of a charismatic experience.

**Q2** Give an example of a mystical experience.

**Q3** What is a conversion experience?

**Q4** What does numinous mean?

ANSWERS

## a direct way in which a believer, or non-believer, can come closer to God

**A1** speaking or singing in tongues, being slain in the spirit, prophecy, words of knowledge

**A2** seeing a vision, hearing God's voice, having a dream with religious significance

**A3** an experience which leads someone to believe in God for the first time, or to change from one religious faith to another

**A4** arousing feelings of awe (holy fear and wonder), a heightened spiritual awareness and a sense of being either very close to God or very separated from him

***examiner's* note** A religious experience need not be dramatic. Some believers would interpret everyday things as a religious experience if they learned more about God through them.

 **ANSWERS**

# Revelation

**Q1** What is general revelation?

**Q2** What is special revelation?

**Q3** How may God be revealed through the lives of religious leaders?

**Q4** How may God be revealed through religious texts?

ANSWERS

# making knowledge of, and from, God known

A1 knowledge and revelation that is available to everyone who seeks it

A2 knowledge and revelation made known to an individual or to a particular group

A3 through the example that they set in their lives; through the work that they do to promote key aspects of biblical teaching; through their charismatic power and authority

A4 they are the most accessible way in which believers can come to know the nature, the will and the plans of God

***examiner's* note** If the Bible is the main source of revelation, then it is important that it is available in as many of the world's languages as possible.

**7 ANSWERS**

# Jesus

**Q1** What place in the Trinity do Christians give to Jesus?

**Q2** What is the incarnation?

**Q3** What do Christians believe about why God sent Jesus to earth?

**Q4** Why is the resurrection of Jesus important to Christians?

ANSWERS

# the central figure in Christian belief

**A1** God the Son

**A2** literally, 'taking on flesh'; Jesus is fully divine, but took on a totally human form to come to earth

**A3** by coming to earth and dying for humanity's sins, Jesus made it possible for humans to re-enter a relationship with God; this relationship had been forfeited in the Garden of Eden

**A4** it proves that he is alive today and can still influence the lives of believers

***examiner's* note** Christians believe that God can be known in the person of Jesus, both when he was on earth, and now, through the Holy Spirit.

# The Holy Spirit

**Q1** When does the Holy Spirit first appear in the Bible?

**Q2** When does Jesus receive the Holy Spirit?

**Q3** What happens at Pentecost (Acts 2)?

**Q4** Why is the Holy Spirit important to Christians?

ANSWERS

**A1** at creation, when God's spirit hovers over the primeval waters and when he breathes his spirit into humanity

**A2** at his baptism

**A3** the disciples receive the Holy Spirit in tongues of fire

**A4** it is the presence of God among his people

***examiner's* note** The Holy Spirit is not a ghost. Although he is not visible or physical, his effects can be experienced in the world and in the lives of Christians.

 **ANSWERS**

# The world around us

**Q1** What does causation mean?

**Q2** What does the Bible teach about the relationship between God and the world?

**Q3** What does design mean?

**Q4** What is the analogy of Paley's Watch?

ANSWERS

## for many Christians, the natural world is the most convincing proof of the existence of God

**A1** everything in the world is caused and so must be caused by something or someone

**A2** God is the supreme creator of all things, out of nothing (*ex nihilo*), (Genesis 1–2)

**A3** everything has an order and a purpose and has not taken the form it has by accident

**A4** William Paley compared a watch with the world: both are designed with accuracy and precision to fulfil a purpose and neither could take the form it does without a designer

***examiner's* note** Thomas Aquinas was one of the most important Christian thinkers to use the causation argument, or Cosmological Argument, for the existence of God.

 **10** ANSWERS

# Science and the Bible

**Q1** Give two reasons why the biblical account of creation is thought to be opposed to a scientific view.

**Q2** What is a liberal view of the biblical account of creation?

**Q3** Why do some Christians find this liberal view challenging?

**Q4** What view does the modern thinker Richard Dawkins hold of the biblical account of creation?

ANSWERS

## the way that the Bible is interpreted can make it more or less compatible with scientific views of the world

**A1** the biblical account describes creation taking place over 6 days, not billions of years; it suggests that animal and human life did not evolve, but was created fully formed; everything is described as 'good', which is a value judgement, not a fact that can be tested

**A2** it illustrates a belief about God's relationship with the world and his intentions for it, but is not an accurate record of how it came about

**A3** they claim that if you question the factual value of any aspect of the Bible, you effectively question it all

**A4** that it is fictional

***examiner's* note** You need to be able to describe briefly the Genesis accounts of creation. Remember there are two accounts — Genesis 1 and Genesis 2 are very different from each other.

 **ANSWERS**

# The origin of the world

**Q1** What is the most commonly accepted scientific view of the origin of the physical world?

**Q2** What is the most commonly accepted scientific view of the origin of animal and human life?

**Q3** What are the key features of the Big Bang theory?

**Q4** What are the key features of the theory of evolution?

ANSWERS ))

# traditionally, religious and scientific views of the world are incompatible

**A1** the Big Bang theory

**A2** natural selection and evolution

**A3** the universe came about through an explosion of matter and energy some 15 billion years ago, but what existed before this is so far unknown

**A4** all living things are descended from common ancestors and each generation has adapted or evolved from more primitive forms of life

***examiner's* note** Do not assume that all Christians and all scientists are opposed to one another. Very often, they are seeking to find an answer which satisfies Christians and scientists alike.

## Atheism

**Q1** Suggest two reasons why someone might not believe in God.

**Q2** What is agnosticism?

**Q3** Why might an atheist use the evidence of religion to count against the existence of God?

**Q4** Is atheism a stronger position to maintain than theism (belief in God)?

ANSWERS

## the view that there is no God

**A1** the existence of God cannot be verified; if God existed there would be no evil and suffering; unanswered prayer; false claims made by others

**A2** the view that since there is no fully reliable evidence for either the existence or non-existence of God, then the only possible position to maintain is that of 'not knowing'

**A3** religion has been taken over by human beings, and can be more to do with power and hypocrisy than worship of God

**A4** not necessarily — if neither believers nor non-believers can see God, then neither can claim they have decisively proved or disproved his existence

***examiner's* note** One atheist theory is that of the psychologist Sigmund Freud, who argued that belief in God is a neurosis.

 **ANSWERS**

# The problem of evil

**Q1** What is the inconsistent triad?

**Q2** What is natural evil?

**Q3** What is moral evil?

**Q4** What is suffering?

ANSWERS

## the challenge to the existence of God posed by the presence of evil in the world

**A1** three contradictory claims — God is all-powerful, God is all-loving, evil exists; all three cannot be true simultaneously

**A2** faults and flaws in the natural world which are beyond human control, e.g. famine, disease, natural disasters and freak weather conditions

**A3** evil actions performed by human beings, and the evil consequences of such actions, e.g. murder, rape, war, theft

**A4** the painful effects of evil, hardship and disaster

***examiner's* note** The problem of evil is often referred to as the problem of suffering. You can understand this by thinking of how evil tends to lead to suffering of some kind.

# Christianity, suffering and evil

**Q1** How might Christians use the Bible to help them cope with the existence of suffering?

**Q2** How might the example of Jesus help Christians who are suffering?

**Q3** Give two beliefs Christians may have about the devil (Satan).

**Q4** Suggest two ways in which Christians might avoid suffering.

ANSWERS

## many believers see suffering as an unavoidable part of Christian life

**A1** the Psalms show that many righteous people suffered and turned to God for support; God sometimes permits suffering for a greater good (the plagues in Egypt), or to test his people (Job)

**A2** Jesus died a humiliating and painful death out of love for humanity, and he is a role model for all believers

**A3** the devil is a real being who is the opposite of God — representing evil rather than good; the devil is a metaphor for evil and has no real existence

**A4** by avoiding temptation; by staying in a relationship with God; by following God's laws

***examiner's* note** Most Christians believe that humans' free will should enable them to make the choice to stay away from evil.

 **ANSWERS**

# Solutions to the problem of evil

**Q1** What is a theodicy?

**Q2** What is purposeful evil?

**Q3** Suggest two solutions Christians may offer to the problem of evil.

**Q4** Propose one criticism for each of these solutions.

ANSWERS ▶▶

# ways in which religious thinkers have tried to solve the challenge that evil poses to the existence of God

**A1** a solution to the problem of evil which does not change the believer's view of God and offers good reasons why God allows evil to exist

**A2** evil that must exist so that certain other conditions, which may be good, may also exist

**A3** evil came into the world when Adam and Eve disobeyed God in the Garden of Eden; without evil we would have no responsibility for each other and no way to make genuinely free choices which please God

**A4** the Garden of Eden narrative is merely a myth and cannot provide real answers; it would be better to have no responsibility if it meant we could not cause harm to others

***examiner's* note** The two classical theodicies offered within Christianity came from Augustine and Irenaeus.

 **ANSWERS**

# Ideas of truth

**Q1** What does empirical mean?

**Q2** What does spiritual mean?

**Q3** Give two examples of questions that religious believers ask about non-physical issues.

**Q4** Why are matters of spiritual truth harder to discuss than matters of empirical truth?

# beliefs about what may be considered to be real or provable

**A1** something that can be made known to the five physical senses

**A2** something that is beyond the physical world, usually associated with religious concepts

**A3** why are we here?; what is the meaning of life?; what happens when we die?; why should we be good?

**A4** they are not supported by physical evidence

***examiner's* note** Think of everyday things that we take for granted which are non-empirical, e.g. the love we feel for other people, our enjoyment of a piece of music. Often they cannot be described in words.

**(17) ANSWERS**

# The role of the Bible

**Q1** Explain the difference between the Old and New Testaments.

**Q2** Why are Christians divided on the authority of the Bible?

**Q3** What kind of literature is included in the Bible?

**Q4** What role does the Bible play in the life of a Christian?

ANSWERS

## the view that the Bible has special status as the word of God

**A1** the Old Testament describes God's dealings with the people of Israel before the coming of Jesus; the New Testament records the life and teaching of Jesus and the early Christian church

**A2** some insist that it is the literal word of God and cannot be reinterpreted to apply to changes in the world; others believe that it was inspired by God, but should be open to human interpretation

**A3** history, poetry, prophecy, letters, gospels, myth, revelation, teaching

**A4** it offers moral guidance, spiritual teaching, information, inspiration and wisdom

***examiner's* note** One of the biggest conflicts between Christians is over the view they take on the nature of the truth contained in the Bible — whether it is literal or spiritual.

**(18) ANSWERS**

# Living the good life

**Q1** What is relative morality?

**Q2** What is absolute morality?

**Q3** Why do Christians think it is important to lead a morally good life?

**Q4** In what ways do Christians believe that God makes humans aware of morality?

ANSWERS

# most Christians believe that there is a relationship between God and morality

**A1** the view that things are right or wrong depending on the situation or culture in which they are done, or their consequences

**A2** the view that things are always right or always wrong, whatever the circumstances

**A3** to set an example to others; to reflect the nature of God and his love; to grow closer to God; to be rewarded on the Day of Judgement

**A4** through the Bible; through revelation and inspiration; through nature; through the conscience; through loving relationships with others

***examiner's* note** The conscience may be understood as the inner guide which tells humans what is right or wrong.

**(19) ANSWERS**

# Christian moral behaviour

**Q1** What is the difference between moral and immoral behaviour?

**Q2** What are the Ten Commandments?

**Q3** What did Jesus mean when he said 'love your neighbour' (Matthew 23:39)?

**Q4** How might conscience help Christians to live in a moral way?

ANSWERS

# how Christians ought to live their lives

**A1** moral behaviour: acting in a way that is good and seen by society as correct; immoral behaviour: acting in a way that others disapprove of

**A2** commandments given by God (Exodus 20) to help people to lead moral lives

**A3** people should love and care for everyone — not just their friends and family

**A4** some Christians believe conscience is like a small voice of God inside us, helping us to choose the right course of action

***examiner's* note** Christians believe that God is a kind of moral law-giver who commands them to do what is right. Therefore they should follow the Bible's teachings. Jesus' main teachings on moral behaviour are in the Sermon on the Mount.

# Moral and immoral occupations

**Q1** Name a moral occupation.

**Q2** Name an immoral occupation.

**Q3** What is the difference between a moral and an immoral occupation?

**Q4** Why should Christians have only moral occupations?

ANSWERS

# jobs that bring good and jobs that bring bad results

**A1** nursing, teaching, caring for others

**A2** drug-dealing, prostitution, pornography, and work that involves exploiting others

**A3** a moral occupation does good to others and has a positive influence on the person doing it; an immoral occupation may harm others and the person doing it

**A4** Christians believe they should use their lives serving God, by behaving and working in morally right ways

***examiner's* note** A consequence of immoral occupations is that people who do them often harm themselves as well as others — for instance, they do things that make them feel bad about who they are and how they behave.

# Use of money

**Q1** What is stewardship?

**Q2** Why is use of money a moral issue for Christians?

**Q3** How may Christians be encouraged to prioritise their use of money?

**Q4** Are Christians required to give up their wealth?

ANSWERS

## the way in which financial resources are used is a matter of moral concern for Christians

A1 exercising responsible care for and use of the resources God has provided

A2 it involves making good and bad choices about use of resources

A3 God first, then the church, then the family

A4 no — only if it is holding them back from a relationship with God, but they should use their wealth wisely and generously

***examiner's* note** Some Christians do choose to give up their wealth and make a commitment to live simply in order to focus on spiritual matters.

# Sin

**Q1** According to the Bible, what brought sin into the world?

**Q2** What is the Fall?

**Q3** What is original sin?

**Q4** What is temptation?

ANSWERS

**A1** humanity's disobedience in the Garden of Eden (Genesis 1–3)

**A2** humanity's loss of perfection after disobeying God's command to eat of the tree of the knowledge of good and evil

**A3** the sin inherited by all humanity from those original human beings who disobeyed God in the Garden of Eden

**A4** the persuasion to perform an action that is unlikely to be in the individual's best interests

***examiner's* note** Some Christians are reluctant to talk about sin in modern teaching, believing it is a concept that increases feelings of unworthiness and can be used to control people.

# Forgiveness

**Q1** What is mercy?

**Q2** What is grace?

**Q3** Why are Christians required to forgive those who have offended them?

**Q4** What does Jesus teach Peter when he asks how many times he should forgive his brother?

ANSWERS

**A1** offering forgiveness and spiritual freedom to individuals who have offended; withholding the punishment they deserve

**A2** undeserved favour and mercy

**A3** in recognition of God's forgiveness of them

**A4** seventy times seven (Matthew 18:17–12) meaning as many times as is necessary, without limit

***examiner's* note** The Bible says that God is just and that he wants all people to live together in justice, peace and fairness: 'Be merciful, just as your Father is merciful' (Luke 6:36).

# Worship and spirituality (1)

**Q1** Give two examples of what might be included in a worship service.

**Q2** How might Christians worship without going to church?

**Q3** In what ways might Christians see their whole lives as acts of worship?

**Q4** What is charismatic worship?

ANSWERS

# acts of praise and dedication to God

**A1** a sermon, prayer, music, sacraments, sharing testimonies

**A2** by praying alone or with other Christians at home, work or school; by telling people about their faith; by reading the Bible and other Christian books; by watching Christian media programmes, especially worship services

**A3** they may believe that everything they do should reflect their belief in God and will be seen by others to do so, e.g. their behaviour at work or socially

**A4** worship led and inspired by the moving of the Holy Spirit

***examiner's* note** Worship is seen as a vital part of Christians' lives. It is something which they do joyfully and which they believe God is pleased to receive.

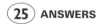

**(25) ANSWERS**

# Worship and spirituality (2)

**Q1** What is corporate worship?

**Q2** What is private worship?

**Q3** What is liturgical worship?

**Q4** Why are festivals important for the spiritual life of Christians?

ANSWERS

# acts of praise and dedication to God

A1 worship conducted in a group, most often in a church

A2 worship conducted by a Christian when alone

A3 worship that follows a set service in church; it has a definite
pattern and worshippers follow carefully; usually based on
written prayers

A4 they form their minds and hearts on key aspects of the life
of Christ and represent a time of mutual celebration
(e.g. Christmas, Easter)

***examiner's* note** Christians may choose to fast in order to dedicate a special
task to God or to pray in a particularly focused way for an unusual event, such
as an evangelistic outreach or a healing.

# Prayer

**Q1** Explain the difference between penitence and petition.

**Q2** Explain the difference between intercession and supplication.

**Q3** What is corporate prayer?

**Q4** Give two reasons why prayer is important to Christians.

ANSWERS

# direct communication with God, either alone or in a group

**A1** penitence means asking for forgiveness; petition means asking for something from God

**A2** intercession means asking God to meet the needs of others; supplication means asking God to meet your own needs

**A3** praying together with other people, either spontaneously or according to a written form of prayer

**A4** it enables them to get close to God; God is a friend and they want to stay in communication with him; it pleases God; it gives God permission to act on their behalf

***examiner's* note** Prayer can also include worship, praise and adoration.

# Food and fasting

**Q1** What is 'fasting'?

**Q2** What is the name of the period in the Christian calendar when a Christian might choose to fast?

**Q3** Why might a Christian fast?

**Q4** Which Christian festival is about giving thanks to God for food?

ANSWERS ▶▶

# the importance of food and fasting in religious belief and practice

A1  going without food as an offering towards God

A2  Lent

A3  to focus the mind on God and show devotion to him; fasting helps to clear the mind and makes the believer more alert to hearing and experiencing God

A4  harvest

***examiner's* note** Although Christians don't have special festival foods, they often eat Simnel cake and hot cross buns at Easter.

# Holy Communion

**Q1** Give two other names used for the Holy Communion service.

**Q2** What does the bread represent?

**Q3** What does the wine represent?

**Q4** On what occasion in the Bible did the sharing of bread and wine first take place?

ANSWERS ▶▶

# a sacramental service in the Christian Church

A1 other names include Mass, Eucharist and the Lord's Supper

A2 the body of Christ

A3 the blood of Christ

A4 Jesus first carried out this ceremony with his disciples at the Last Supper, on the night before he was crucified (Luke 22:17–24)

*examiner's* **note** Mass is a term used by the Roman Catholic Church, and Eucharist (meaning 'thanksgiving'), is widely used in other denominations, particularly in the Anglican Church.

# Christian symbols

**Q1** What symbols do Christians use to represent the Holy Spirit?

**Q2** Identify two symbols used to describe Jesus and his role.

**Q3** What symbols are used in Holy Communion or Mass?

**Q4** How might Christians use symbols in worship?

ANSWERS

## visual or linguistic means of representing Christian concepts beyond the physical world

A1 fire, breath, wind, dove, water

A2 a shepherd, the true vine, the bread of life, light of the world, the gate for the sheep, the lamb of God

A3 bread (a wafer or real bread) and wine (or a non-alcoholic substitute) represent the body and blood of Jesus

A4 to help them meditate on the meaning of what the symbols represent; to aid their understanding; to explain the meaning of Christian beliefs to others

*examiner's* note The Bible is full of symbolic language about God, e.g. 'Blessed be the Lord, my rock…my fortress…my shield in whom I take refuge' (Psalm 144:1–2).

# Christian music and art

**Q1** Why is a picture of a fish important to Christians?

**Q2** Why is music important to most forms of Christian worship?

**Q3** What different views do Christians have on the use of music?

**Q4** What different views do Christians have on the use of religious art?

**ANSWERS**

# Christian culture has led to many great works of religious art and music

**A1** it was used to identify Christian groups in times of persecution and some modern Christians use it to identify themselves as believers

**A2** it gives back to God the talents he has bestowed; it helps to focus the worshipper's mind on key beliefs; it encourages people to join together in worship; it is inspiring

**A3** some fear that it encourages showing off and can be distracting; others place it at the heart of a service of worship and encourage everyone to make a musical contribution

**A4** some believe it is part of a tradition of helping people to understand the gospel; others fear that it might encourage idolatry or be too secular

***examiner's* note** Charismatic worship places music at its centre; Roman Catholic churches usually feature more art than Protestant churches.

 **ANSWERS**

# Ecumenism

**Q1** What is the ecumenical movement?

**Q2** When did it begin?

**Q3** What is the World Council of Churches?

**Q4** Why do some people think that ecumenism is a failure?

ANSWERS

**A1** an attempt to get the various Christian churches to work together

**A2** 1910

**A3** an association of Christian churches who are trying to spread the same message of Christianity throughout the world

**A4** some say it has been a failure because the Roman Catholic Church has not become involved at a deep level

***examiner's* note** A difficult topic — try to remember that it is not about all Christians belonging to one big church. Ecumenism is about getting churches to work together, while keeping their own identity.

# The sanctity of life

**Q1** What does sacred mean?

**Q2** How might Christians use the creation narratives to support their belief in the sanctity of life?

**Q3** How does the life of Jesus support the principle of the sanctity of life?

**Q4** What does Paul mean when he describes the body as 'the temple of the Holy Spirit' (1 Corinthians 6:19)?

ANSWERS

# human life has special value and worth

A1 holy or set apart for God's purposes

A2 human life is the climax and focus of creation, made by God in an especially personal way

A3 God himself became human in the person of Jesus Christ

A4 the human body is not simply a physical object, it is the dwelling place of the Holy Spirit, which comes from God and must be treated with reverence and respect

*examiner's* **note** Christians believe that humans were created in the image of God (Genesis 1:27), which gives them a special value in creation.

(33) **ANSWERS**

# Judgements about human life

**Q1** What is a relative judgement?

**Q2** What is an absolute judgement?

**Q3** What is a value judgement?

**Q4** Why might some Christians say that it is wrong to make judgements about quality of life?

ANSWERS

# assessing whether a person's life is valuable

A1 a judgement which may be different in different situations

A2 a judgement which is always the same in every situation

A3 a judgement about the quality or worth of something rather than a statement about facts

A4 everyone has different values; physical disabilities may lead to judgements about the whole person; humans tend to place too much emphasis on ideas of perfection

***examiner's* note** You need to understand that these are issues of morality which reflect the fact that humans have many different moral opinions.

# Protecting human life

**Q1** Which of the Ten Commandments establishes the value of human life?

**Q2** Give two situations in which the application of this commandment may be difficult.

**Q3** What does the phrase 'quality of life' refer to?

**Q4** Suggest two ways in which someone's quality of life might be evaluated.

ANSWERS

# Christians believe that human life should be protected because it is sacred

A1 'You shall not murder' (Exodus 20:13)

A2 abortion, self-defence, war, capital punishment

A3 those things which make life enjoyable and meaningful

A4 health and physical fitness, ability to communicate or do things which are important to the individual, e.g. to work, relate to loved ones, pursue interests

***examiner's* note** Remember that the commandment is not 'You shall not kill', although it has traditionally been translated in that way.

# Personhood

**Q1** What is a person?

**Q2** At what stages might human life be said to begin?

**Q3** How might we identify someone as a person?

**Q4** Suggest one situation in which religious believers are concerned about personhood.

ANSWERS

# the defining character of a human being

A1  a human being

A2  at the moment of fertilisation; at the moment when the fertilised egg is implanted into the wall of the womb; at the moment when the foetus moves in the womb; at the point when the foetus could exist independently of the mother

A3  by their physical appearance; by their personality; by their thinking processes; by their ability to communicate; by their ability to feel pain and express emotion

A4  when deciding whether to: have an abortion; let a terminally sick baby die; withdraw treatment from a terminally sick adult

***examiner's* note** Personal identity is important for Christians because they believe that God created every individual for a unique purpose.

# Abortion

**Q1** What are the legally permissible reasons for abortion in the UK?

**Q2** What is the latest date for an abortion, except in exceptional cases?

**Q3** Why might a woman claim that she has the right to an abortion?

**Q4** What is meant by pro-life, and by pro-choice?

ANSWERS

# the termination of a pregnancy

A1  if the mother's life is at risk; if the mother's physical or mental
    health is at risk; if the child might be born severely handicapped;
    if there is a risk to the health of the mother's other children

A2  24 weeks

A3  she has the right to make choices concerning her body, her life,
    her future and her fertility

A4  the view that life is intrinsically valuable and should be protected;
    the view that women have a right to choose an abortion

***examiner's* note** Abortions were legalised under the 1967 Abortion Act
(amended 1990).

# Abortion — religious views

**Q1** Suggest two religious objections to abortion.

**Q2** Suggest two reasons that a religious believer might give for permitting an abortion.

**Q3** Which groups of Christians are most likely to be opposed to abortion?

**Q4** Why are pro-life advocates sometimes accused of using emotive language?

**ANSWERS**

## in principle, the Christian church is opposed to abortion

A1 the sanctity of life; the Bible forbids the murder of human beings; life begins at the moment of conception; the foetus is created in the image of God; every human being has the right to life

A2 possibly in cases of rape or incest, or where the trauma to the mother will outweigh the good done by having the child

A3 Roman Catholics and evangelical Protestants

A4 they often refer to the foetus as the 'unborn child'

***examiner's* note** Search the internet for anti-abortion websites and evaluate the methods they use to convey their message.

(38) ANSWERS

# Euthanasia

**Q1** What is passive euthanasia?

**Q2** What is active euthanasia?

**Q3** What is voluntary euthanasia?

**Q4** What is assisted suicide?

ANSWERS

the termination of the life of someone suffering from great physical or mental handicap or a painful illness

A1 where medical treatment to prolong a patient's life is no longer given and the patient is allowed to die naturally

A2 where a doctor actively ends the life of a patient, e.g. by lethal injection

A3 where a doctor deliberately ends the life of a patient at his/her request

A4 providing the means for someone to commit suicide

*examiner's* note Make sure you are clear about these definitions as it is easy to get them mixed up and to lose vital marks.

# Arguments in favour of euthanasia

**Q1** What is the death with dignity argument?

**Q2** What is the quality of life argument?

**Q3** What is the economics argument?

**Q4** What is the compassion argument?

ANSWERS

# despite the difficulties, many people would support the legalisation of euthanasia

A1 it would allow sufferers to die with dignity rather than dying a slow death where their physical and mental condition may increasingly deteriorate and they may suffer considerably

A2 although the best medical care may keep people alive for longer, their quality of life may be poor, e.g. keeping them free from pain by use of drugs may leave them permanently semi-conscious; in such cases there may be an argument for euthanasia

A3 it would save on hospital and medical expenses and make more beds available for non-terminal patients

A4 it leads to a gentle, pain-free death

***examiner's* note** Euthanasia may also be favoured because it relieves the burden on families who might otherwise have to go to great trouble and expense.

# Euthanasia — religious views

**Q1** Why might some Christians believe that suffering and illness may be valuable?

**Q2** What might Christians suggest could reduce the need for euthanasia?

**Q3** Suggest a social argument that religious believers could offer against euthanasia.

**Q4** Why might Christians claim that humans should not be able to choose when they die?

ANSWERS

## most religious believers think it is wrong to take any action to kill a patient, even if it relieves suffering

A1 they may believe that all suffering should be seen as part of a test and euthanasia amounts to a refusal to accept the trials which play an important part in building an individual's relationship with God

A2 more hospices — residential homes where those suffering a terminal illness can live out their remaining days being cared for in a peaceful and dignified way

A3 if doctors are allowed to kill those who are very sick, then it is conceivable that society will stop looking for cures in such cases

A4 life is regarded as a gift from God, which only he can take away

***examiner's* note** Sometimes the only way to ease a person's pain is to give them large doses of painkillers that, in the end, may kill them anyway. This is an example of 'double effect'.

 **ANSWERS**

# Terminal care

**Q1** What does it mean to say someone is 'terminally ill'?

**Q2** What is palliative care?

**Q3** What is a hospice?

**Q4** Why might Christians encourage better palliative care for patients with terminal illness?

ANSWERS

# care of sick people in the final stages of life

A1 the person will die from the illness

A2 care for patients focused on relieving pain rather than curing the illness

A3 a medical institution that cares for dying and terminally ill people, with the focus on palliative care

A4 because it discourages thoughts of euthanasia

***examiner's* note** 'We are now always able to control pain in terminal cancer in the patients sent to us...euthanasia as advocated is wrong...it should be unnecessary and is an admission of defeat' (Christian Hospice Movement).

# Suicide

**Q1** What is the status of suicide according to the law?

**Q2** Give two arguments raised by Christians regarding suicide.

**Q3** What support might be given to people contemplating suicide?

**Q4** What well-known organisation exists primarily to help potential suicide victims?

ANSWERS

# self-killing

A1 it is no longer illegal in the UK, although it was until 1961

A2 it is a rejection of God's gift of life; it is murder of the self and the Bible forbids murder; it is an irrational act; it is selfish, uncaring and irresponsible

A3 pain management, counselling, prayer, practical support to deal with problems which may lead to suicide — debt, loneliness, bereavement

A4 the Samaritans, founded in 1953

***examiner's* note** Most Christians would be concerned not to encourage the traditional view that people who commit suicide go straight to hell.

 **ANSWERS**

# Fertility treatment

**Q1** What is IVF?

**Q2** What is surrogacy?

**Q3** In Britain, what happens to unused embryos from IVF?

**Q4** What is so controversial about surrogacy?

ANSWERS

# methods which enable infertile men and women to have children

A1  *in vitro* fertilisation — resulting babies are often referred to as test-tube babies

A2  when a woman bears a child on behalf of another woman, with the intention that she will hand it over to her at the end of the pregnancy

A3  they are destroyed — this is an issue of great controversy

A4  it may create an unnaturally close relationship between either partner and the surrogate; either party might go back on the agreement; the child may later have difficulty with the notion of being born through a surrogate

***examiner's* note** IVF and surrogacy are controversial because they are not only expensive, but also cause dilemmas over natural parentage and children's right to know who their natural parents really are.

 **ANSWERS**

# Issues regarding fertility

**Q1** What is AID or AIH?

**Q2** What do some Christians think is a better alternative to fertility treatment?

**Q3** Why are Christians divided on the issue of fertility treatment?

**Q4** Why might some Christians choose not to have children?

**ANSWERS**

# some methods of conceiving children cause moral and social dilemmas

A1 'artificial insemination by donor' or 'artificial insemination by husband'

A2 adoption — this gives a home to a child who needs to be wanted

A3 some Christians believe that God would bless any efforts made to conceive; others suggest that infertile couples should accept it is God's will for them not to have children

A4 they may wish to dedicate themselves more effectively to Christian work, possibly as missionaries or other full-time Christian workers

***examiner's* note** There are many moral questions about fertility treatment, including the problem of what happens to fertilised eggs which are not subsequently used.

 **ANSWERS**

# Genetic engineering

**Q1** What is positive eugenics?

**Q2** What is negative eugenics?

**Q3** What is cloning?

**Q4** Why are some Christians troubled by genetic engineering?

ANSWERS

# the use of scientific methods to determine the characteristics of a foetus

A1 using genetics to engineer a foetus with specially selected, desirable features, e.g. high IQ, perfect eyesight

A2 using genetics to eliminate negative traits, e.g. a predisposition to heart disease, alcoholism

A3 creating genetic replicas of humans, animals, organs or body parts

A4 it places authority over life and death in human hands; humans may become more demanding and may consider many people 'imperfect'

***examiner's* note** The film *Gattaca* is set in a future state in which it is the norm to be genetically engineered — it addresses many important moral questions.

# Animal life

**Q1** Explain how Christians might explain the difference between human and animal life.

**Q2** What activities by humans might show that they regard themselves as having authority over animals?

**Q3** How might Christians express a belief that animal life should be treated with respect?

**Q4** Why might some Christians object to the methods adopted by some animal rights activists?

ANSWERS ▶▶

# the status of non-human animals is a religious, ethical and political issue

A1 by making reference to the creation account in which humans are given authority over the animals

A2 eating meat; keeping pets; supporting circuses; using animals for experimentation

A3 by being vegetarian; by working for animal charities; by using products not tested on animals

A4 they sometimes use violence

***examiner's* note** Some Christians may claim that although it is important not to be cruel to animals, human life should always take precedence.

# Animal testing

**Q1** For what reasons may animals be used in medical research?

**Q2** For what other purposes may animals be used in research?

**Q3** Why do Christians have divided views about the use of animals in medical research?

**Q4** Give one objection to animal testing and one view in support of it.

**ANSWERS** ▶▶

# the use of non-human animals in scientific research

A1 testing new medications in their early stages; developing new possibilities in organ transplants; psychological and behavioural tests; developing fertility treatment; genetic engineering

A2 developing biological weaponry; testing cosmetics and other products

A3 some believe that animals are for human use and have no objection to them being experimented on for medical purposes; others claim that the principle of the sanctity of life extends to animals and they should be protected from experimentation

A4 it violates the rights of animals to live free from pain (against); improving the quality of human life justifies animal suffering (for)

***examiner's* note** The biblical concept of stewardship — care for the environment — may be extended to include care for animals.

# Body and soul

**Q1** What is dualism?

**Q2** What is monism?

**Q3** How does a belief in dualism influence views on life after death?

**Q4** How does belief in the resurrection of Jesus influence views on the afterlife?

ANSWERS

# the two aspects of human nature, the physical and non-physical

A1 the view that human nature is of two natures — physical and non-physical

A2 the view that human nature is a psycho-physical unity

A3 it suggests that, although the body dies, the spirit can live on

A4 Jesus was fully restored to life and appeared in bodily form, suggesting that believers can look forward to a replicated body in the afterlife

***examiner's* note** Jesus' resurrection was different, however, from what may be expected in the afterlife, since he was restored to life on earth, ascending later to a heavenly place.

# Life after death (1)

**Q1** Suggest two reasons why Christians believe in life after death.

**Q2** Why might a non-religious person believe in an afterlife?

**Q3** What does the resurrection of Jesus teach about the afterlife?

**Q4** Suggest two other ways in which humans may experience an afterlife.

ANSWERS

A1  God's plan for humanity does not end with death; God's love continues after death; God has the power to raise the dead; an afterlife is necessary for divine punishment and reward

A2  it is difficult to believe that this life is all there is; people feel that there ought to be something beyond earthly life that gives meaning to life; earthly life is short, so an afterlife may be the place where humanity can fulfil its potential

A3  the death and resurrection of Jesus Christ are proof that there is life beyond the grave

A4  immortality of the soul; reincarnation

**examiner's note** It is not necessary to have religious beliefs to look forward to an afterlife, but most Christians claim that only God could bring it about.

# Life after death (2)

**Q1** Why do some people reject a belief in life after death?

**Q2** In what ways might non-religious people believe that life goes on beyond the grave?

**Q3** What is a near-death experience?

**Q4** What is the paranormal?

**ANSWERS**

# living on in some form after the death of the physical body

A1  there is no physical proof; it is a logically impossible idea; it is an undesirable prospect

A2  people's creations have significance and their fame lives on; we prolong our lives in the lives of our children and in the memories of others; we may live on as a supernatural essence of some kind

A3  an experience after clinical death when a patient may see bright lights or a religious figure, before being sent back to earth

A4  experiences that suggest that there may be a non-visible, spirit world, e.g. ghosts, communications through mediums

**examiner's note** Most Christians would not attempt to contact the dead. God condemned Saul, the first king of Israel, for doing so (1 Samuel 28).

 **ANSWERS**

# Christian beliefs about the afterlife

**Q1** What is heaven?

**Q2** Give two examples of ways in which Christians might understand hell.

**Q3** What opposing beliefs might Christians have about who goes to heaven?

**Q4** What is the Day of Judgement?

ANSWERS ▶▶

## many Christians believe that the afterlife is lived in heaven or hell

A1 a place or state of everlasting joy, spent in the presence of God

A2 some believe that it is a literal place of punishment; others believe that it represents symbolically the absence of God

A3 evangelical Christians believe that only those who have been born again or who accept Jesus as their personal saviour can go to heaven, but many Christians are more inclusive and suggest that eventually everyone may reach heaven

A4 the day at the end of time when all people will stand before God's throne and be judged for their beliefs and their works

*examiner's* note A useful word to know is 'eschatology' — it refers to beliefs about the events associated with the end of time, such as judgement, salvation, heaven and hell.

# Punishment and reward in the afterlife

**Q1** Why do some Christians believe that it is fair to expect to be punished or rewarded in the afterlife?

**Q2** Give one argument against the view expressed in Q1.

**Q3** What do some Christians believe about the relationship between God, morality and the afterlife?

**Q4** What do Christians mean by salvation?

ANSWERS

# punishment and reward is a possible purpose of an afterlife

A1 humans beings have free will and make rational choices about their behaviour, so they should be accountable for it

A2 we do not have genuine free will; it is a matter of opinion as to what is deserving of punishment or reward; it is an out-of-date view of the afterlife

A3 because God is the maker of moral laws, then he must exist to carry out rewards and punishments in the afterlife

A4 the belief that Jesus' death will save them from being punished for their sins

***examiner's note*** These are difficult ideas which people take very personally and seriously. It is important to recognise that not all Christians are in agreement on them.

# Funerals

**Q1** What is a cremation?

**Q2** What is the difference between a funeral and a memorial service?

**Q3** What is meant by the phrase 'ashes to ashes, dust to dust'?

**Q4** Suggest two ways in which funerals are important to the bereaved.

**ANSWERS**

# a rite of passage to mark the end of a person's life

A1 where the body and the coffin are burnt to ashes — the ashes may later be scattered or kept in an urn as a memorial

A2 a funeral follows an order of service committing the soul of the deceased to God; a memorial service celebrates the life of the deceased and may take place some time after death

A3 it refers to the words of Genesis 3:19 — man was created from the earth and will return to it when he dies and his body decays

A4 they help the bereaved to mourn; they are a time to say goodbye to the deceased; religious funerals reflect belief in the afterlife; they honour the memory of the deceased

***examiner's* note** A funeral may have no religious content at all and funeral services can be designed around the life and character of the person who has died.

# Issues regarding sex

**Q1** What is pre-marital sex?

**Q2** What is the only one of the Ten Commandments to deal with sexual relationships?

**Q3** What is monogamy?

**Q4** What is polygamy?

ANSWERS

# Christians believe it is important to remain committed to one sexual partner

A1 sex before marriage

A2 do not commit adultery (Exodus 20:14)

A3 having one marriage partner

A4 having more than one marriage partner

***examiner's* note** Adultery and promiscuity are not against the law in the UK. In Islamic countries which operate under the Shariah law they are, in some cases, punishable by death.

# Issues regarding sexual relationships

**Q1** What is the Civil Partnership Act 2005?

**Q2** What is adultery?

**Q3** What is celibacy?

**Q4** Does the Bible encourage everyone to marry?

ANSWERS

## some Christians consider certain types of sexual behaviour to be morally and spiritually wrong

A1  the Act that provided for the legalisation of same-sex partnerships

A2  when a married person has sex with someone other than his or her partner

A3  a commitment to resist sexual relationships — in the Roman Catholic church priests are expected to remain celibate and not to marry

A4  no — Paul writes that those who remain celibate may find the Christian life easier (1 Corinthians 7)

***examiner's* note** To our knowledge, Jesus never married.

# Marriage and the Bible

**Q1** How does the Bible define marriage?

**Q2** According to the New Testament, what must a husband do for his wife?

**Q3** What does the New Testament teach that a wife must do?

**Q4** What position of authority, according to Paul, does a husband have over his wife?

ANSWERS

A1  a union ordained by God (Mark 10:7–9)

A2  love her as himself (Ephesians 5:33)

A3  respect her husband (Ephesians 5:33)

A4  the husband is the head of the wife (Ephesians 5:23)

***examiner's* note** The Bible uses the notion of *agape* when talking about love in marriage — it means loving someone without asking for anything in return. The most important illustration of *agape* love is Jesus' death on the cross as a sacrifice to save humanity.

# Christian beliefs regarding marriage

**Q1** What does Paul teach about sexual relationships within marriage?

**Q2** What is the traditional reason for marriage within the Christian Church?

**Q3** What other reasons for marriage may be offered by Christians?

**Q4** What does the Roman Catholic Church teach about sex within marriage?

ANSWERS ▶▶

# Christians hold marriage to be a vitally important institution on which the well-being of the family is based

A1 'the wife's body does not belong to her alone, but also to her husband. In the same way, the husband's body does not belong to him alone but also to his wife' (1 Corinthians 7:4)

A2 to have children: 'For this reason, a man will leave his father and mother and be united to his wife, and they will become one flesh' (Genesis 2:24)

A3 'marriage is given, that husband and wife may comfort and help each other, living faithfully together in need and in plenty, in sorrow and in joy...' (Church of England marriage service)

A4 'the sexual act must take place exclusively within marriage. Outside marriage it always constitutes a grave sin' (The Catechism of the Catholic Church)

***examiner's* note** Marriage is the lifelong union of two people that can be ended only by the death of one partner, or by divorce.

# The Christian marriage service

**Q1** What word means making a promise before God in a wedding ceremony?

**Q2** What do the couple pray for at a wedding service?

**Q3** Why is the marriage service sometimes called a 'sacrament'?

**Q4** Which other sacrament may the newly married couple share during the service?

ANSWERS

# a religious service uniting a couple

A1 vow

A2 they ask for God's blessing on their relationship

A3 it is a ceremony in which the church confers God's love and grace on believers

A4 Holy Communion

***examiner's* note** In the marriage service great emphasis is put on faithfulness — the belief that, once married, a couple should commit themselves, sexually and emotionally, wholly to each other.

# Wedding ceremonies

**Q1** How are weddings that take place in a church usually described?

**Q2** Where do most non-church weddings take place?

**Q3** What are non-church wedding ceremonies called?

**Q4** Why do couples traditionally exchange rings?

ANSWERS ▶▶

A1 religious wedding ceremonies

A2 at a register office or other place licensed for weddings

A3 civil marriage ceremonies

A4 as a sign of the everlasting nature of their relationship

***examiner's* note** A couple do not have to be religious believers in order to marry in a Protestant church, although they are generally expected to attend the church for 6 weeks before the wedding. For Roman Catholic ceremonies, at least one of the couple has to be a practising Catholic.

# Cohabitation

**Q1** Suggest a social reason why a couple might cohabit.

**Q2** What is a trial marriage?

**Q3** Does the Bible support cohabitation?

**Q4** Why do some Christians cohabit?

 ANSWERS **))**

A1 sexual relationships before and outside marriage have become increasingly acceptable; one partner is not yet divorced

A2 living with someone before marriage in order to see if you get on with him or her

A3 it is implicitly discouraged since it is likely to involve sex outside marriage

A4 they think that it helps to develop a strong relationship before entering into the commitment of marriage

***examiner's* note** In 1995 the Church of England published a report entitled 'Something to Celebrate', which offered support to the notion of cohabitation.

# Divorce

**Q1** On what grounds is divorce permitted in the UK?

**Q2** Give three ways in which these grounds might be proved.

**Q3** Why may divorce have increased in the modern world?

**Q4** What is remarriage?

ANSWERS

A1 when a marriage has irretrievably broken down

A2 adultery, unreasonable behaviour, separation, desertion

A3 people live longer; women are not financially dependent on men

A4 marrying again after divorce to a new partner or to the previous marriage partner

**examiner's note** In 1936 Edward VIII had to give up the throne because he wanted to marry a divorced woman, Mrs Wallis Simpson.

# Divorce — religious views

**Q1** Why do many Christians oppose divorce?

**Q2** Can a divorced Christian remarry in church?

**Q3** What is an annulment?

**Q4** Give two grounds for an annulment.

ANSWERS

A1 it breaks promises made before God and to another human being

A2 a Protestant can, with permission of the minister; a Roman Catholic generally cannot

A3 it is where a marriage is dissolved because, legally speaking, its conditions were not fulfilled

A4 if the couple were under age; if, due to diminished responsibility, the couple did not know what they were doing; if the marriage was not consummated; if one or both partners were coerced into the marriage

***examiner's* note** The teaching of Jesus concerning divorce is ambiguous. In Mark 10:11–12 Jesus prohibits divorce, but in Matthew 5:32 Jesus appears to allow divorce on grounds of marital unfaithfulness.

 **ANSWERS**

# Homosexuality

**Q1** What is the age of consent for homosexuals in the UK?

**Q2** What does heterosexuality mean?

**Q3** What is lesbianism?

**Q4** Why are many Christians opposed to homosexuality?

ANSWERS

A1 16

A2 sexual attraction to members of the opposite sex

A3 sexual attraction between women

A4 several Old Testament and New Testament teachings appear to be opposed to it, e.g. Leviticus 18:22, Romans 1:26–27

***examiner's* note** Although the UK does not allow homosexual marriages, churches may be prepared to give a service of blessing on long-term homosexual relationships.

# Homosexuality and the church

**Q1** What does the Roman Catholic church teach concerning homosexuality?

**Q2** Are practising homosexuals allowed to become priests in the Protestant church?

**Q3** Suggest two reasons why no teaching of Jesus on homosexuality is recorded in the New Testament.

**Q4** What is the GCM?

ANSWERS

## homosexuality is one of the greatest areas of controversy in the Christian church today

A1  homosexual orientation not a sin; homosexuals should stay celibate

A2  yes, if they are strongly supported by their bishop and the local congregation — but most evangelical Protestants do not agree, as they see homosexuality as a sin which can be cured through prayer

A3  he accepted the Jewish teaching on it and did not engage in debate with the Pharisees on the matter; he did not want to encourage discrimination against homosexuals so did not address the issue; he did not address sexism either, but taught women alongside men

A4  Gay Christian Movement: an organisation supporting the role and rights of homosexuals within the church

*examiner's* note There is much controversy surrounding the meaning of biblical phrases such as those in Genesis 19:5 and 1 Corinthians 6:9.

 **65** ANSWERS

# Contraception

**Q1** Name two forms of artificial contraception.

**Q2** Name one form of permanent contraception.

**Q3** Why does the Roman Catholic church oppose artificial contraception?

**Q4** What type of contraception is acceptable to the Roman Catholic church?

ANSWERS

# the deliberate prevention of pregnancy

A1 the pill, condom, IUD, morning-after pill

A2 sterilisation, vasectomy

A3 it prevents the transmission of life, which is against God's commandment in Genesis 1:28

A4 the natural or rhythm method

***examiner's* note** Roman Catholics oppose the morning-after pill because they claim it acts after conception has taken place. The natural method is acceptable because it allows sex to occur at a time when the woman is least likely to conceive.

# Family

**Q1** What is a nuclear family? What is a reconstituted family?

**Q2** What is an extended family? What is a single parent family?

**Q3** Which of the Ten Commandments is concerned with the family?

**Q4** Why does the Bible highlight the importance of the family?

ANSWERS

# a primary social group consisting of parents and their offspring

A1 two parents living together with their children; where two families broken by divorce or death become one new family unit

A2 parents, children and other relatives living together or in close proximity; where one parent has sole care of his/her children

A3 'Honour your father and your mother' (Exodus 20:12)

A4 the family is the setting where children can grow up secure in the knowledge and love of God

***examiner's* note** The fastest-growing type of family today is the single-parent family. This is due to the increase in the divorce rate and to more women choosing to have a child without a permanent partner.

# Roles of men and women in the family

**Q1** What might a Christian believe to be the traditional roles of men and women within the family?

**Q2** What changes in society have affected these traditional roles?

**Q3** How might a Christian father fulfil a traditional role today?

**Q4** How might a Christian mother fulfil a traditional role today?

**ANSWERS** ))

# many Christians try to maintain a traditional view of the family unit

A1 men support the family financially and women provide care within the home

A2 changes in working patterns; an increase in single-parent families; a greater emphasis on sexual equality

A3 by providing religious teaching for his children; by ensuring it is financially possible for his wife not to have to work outside the home; by supporting and encouraging his wife and children

A4 by being at home with pre-school children and when the children return from school; by showing respect towards her husband; by praying with her children

***examiner's* note** These are subjective issues. Your answers should not suggest that it is morally wrong not to fulfil these traditional roles.

# Family and the church

**Q1** How might the church help to support a Christian family?

**Q2** How does the church provide religious teaching to families?

**Q3** How is the church a model of the family unit?

**Q4** How should the church emulate Jesus in its attitude to the family?

ANSWERS

# the church itself is regarded as a family of believers

A1  by providing support during illness, bereavement, unemployment, family separation; by being non-judgemental and caring

A2  through Sunday school, youth groups, Alpha courses and other Bible study groups, women's and men's groups

A3  all the members are united by being children of God

A4  by showing *agape* love

***examiner's* note** Some Christians are disappointed when their church is critical of their family circumstances at times when they most need help and support.

# Family and social trends

**Q1** In what ways has the family been influenced by changes in society?

**Q2** In what ways has the Civil Partnerships Act changed family trends?

**Q3** Why might Christian beliefs have less influence on family life today?

**Q4** In what ways has life for children within the family changed in recent years?

**ANSWERS**

# the UK family has seen many changes in recent decades

A1 the UK has become a multi-faith and multi-ethnic society; people are more tolerant of others' views; the Church is less influential; it is acceptable for a couple to live together without being married (cohabitation); the status of women has changed

A2 same-sex couples may now adopt children, as well as have a child biologically related to at least one partner

A3 they might seem irrelevant to a predominantly secular or multi-religious society

A4 children have more personal spending money; are allowed more social freedom; more have sexual relationships before leaving school; they share less time with their parents

***examiner's* note** In 1980, 12% of children were born outside marriage; it is 42% today.

 **ANSWERS**

# Social harmony

**Q1** For what reason may some Christians believe that the law will never stop prejudice?

**Q2** Why do some Christians claim that it is impossible to achieve true equality in society?

**Q3** How might a Christian argue against the view that there will be no harmony until everyone shares the same religious beliefs?

**Q4** How may Christians respond to the claim that people shouldn't be treated in the same way because they are unique?

ANSWERS

# when people live together in a peaceful society without division

A1 because the law may make something an offence, but it won't necessarily change people's attitudes

A2 because society consists of individuals who are so different that they cannot practically be treated in the same way

A3 because even if people don't share a religious faith they should share the view that all humanity is of equal importance

A4 they would value and respect a person's individuality, but at the same time they would believe in equality of human rights and opportunities for all individuals

***examiner's* note** There are no right answers to these kinds of questions, but you must provide clear reasons for the answers that you give.

**(71) ANSWERS**

# Fighting injustice

**Q1** What was unusual about Jesus' group of followers?

**Q2** Which German theologian was sent to a concentration camp for opposing the Nazis?

**Q3** What is a prisoner of conscience?

**Q4** Which charity works to support prisoners of conscience?

ANSWERS

A1 it included several women (Luke 8:1–3); there is plenty of evidence that women played a significant role in the ministry of Jesus and the early church, and that wealthy women provided for the financial needs of its leaders

A2 Dietrich Bonhoeffer

A3 someone who is imprisoned for the ideological beliefs they hold

A4 Amnesty International

**examiner's note** Don't assume that religious believers conform to the rules of society all the time. Many have suffered death for standing up against society's injustices.

# Gender issues in the past

**Q1** With what women's rights organisation is Emmeline Pankhurst associated?

**Q2** In 1900, what percentage of married women went to work outside the home: 15%, 20% or 25%?

**Q3** How did the two world wars change the status of women?

**Q4** In what year were women over 21 granted the right to vote?

ANSWERS

A1 the Suffragettes; the movement fought vigorously for the right for women to vote

A2 15%

A3 more women entered the workplace to take over jobs performed by men who had been drafted into military service

A4 1928

***examiner's* note** Many women feel that there is still an inherent bias towards men in the worlds of work, home and society, and that the fight for equality is not over. The suffragettes have been viewed as the forerunners of the modern feminist movement.

# Gender issues today

**Q1** What is sexism?

**Q2** What is sexual equality?

**Q3** What was made illegal by the Sex Discrimination Act?

**Q4** What was the EPA and how did it improve the status of women?

ANSWERS

## women and men are protected by law against overt acts of sexual discrimination and sexual harassment

A1  discriminating against people because of their gender

A2  the belief that the sexes are equal

A3  discrimination in employment on the grounds of sex or marital status

A4  the Equal Pay Act — it gave women the same pay as men for doing the same job

***examiner's* note** The cultural attitudes of the different faith groups in the UK have a considerable influence on the way the status of women is viewed in certain communities.

# Gender issues and the Bible

**Q1** What does the Bible say about the creation of women?

**Q2** Why are women significant in the accounts of the resurrection of Jesus?

**Q3** Why is the biblical teaching on marriage seen by some to give men the dominant role?

**Q4** According to Paul, what must a woman do in church?

ANSWERS

## the Bible has apparent contradictions — women are equal, yet in some places men appear to be dominant

**A1** Genesis 1:27 says women were created at the same time as men and both are made in God's image; Genesis 2:22 describes woman as being formed by God out of the rib of the man

**A2** in all the gospel accounts it is women who see the risen Christ first

**A3** Ephesians 5:23 says that the husband is the 'head' of the wife — although some interpret this as giving him responsibility, others interpret it as giving him power

**A4** be silent (1 Timothy 2:11–12; 1 Corinthians 14:34)

***examiner's* note** Jesus treated men and women equally. Many of the texts which appear to suggest male dominance are written by Paul and do not come from Jesus' own ministry.

 **ANSWERS**

# Ordination of women

**Q1** Can a woman become a priest in the Roman Catholic church?

**Q2** In what year did the Church of England first allow the ordination of women as priests?

**Q3** Why do many Christians oppose the ordination of women?

**Q4** What may be the advantages of having women priests?

ANSWERS

## the appointment of women to positions of official leadership in the church

A1 no — the teaching of the Roman Catholic church is that only a baptised male can receive ordination

A2 1994

A3 the teaching of Paul in 1 Corinthians 14:34 and 1 Timothy 2:12; Jesus chose 12 men to be apostles

A4 women may be seen as less authoritarian and more compassionate, loving and sympathetic

*examiner's* note Several non-denominational and non-conformist churches have had women in leadership positions for many years.

# Race and the Bible

**Q1** What does the Bible teach about race?

**Q2** Which famous parable of Jesus deals with racism?

**Q3** According to Paul, what promises do believers of all races share?

**Q4** What does the so-called 'golden rule' have to teach about the relationship between races?

ANSWERS

## the Bible condemns racism and urges believers to seek racial harmony

A1 all races are created equally, e.g. Acts 10:34–35, Galatians 3:28

A2 the good Samaritan

A3 the promises God made to Abraham in Genesis 12:3 (Galatians 3:29)

A4 'In everything do to others as you would have them do to you' (Matthew 7:12)

*examiner's* **note** The Methodist church states: 'We affirm that racism is a direct contradiction of the gospel of Jesus.'

(77) ANSWERS

# Racial issues

**Q1** What is racial prejudice?

**Q2** Why is the UK said to be a multi-ethnic society?

**Q3** What is racial discrimination?

**Q4** Why did so many immigrants enter the UK in the 1950s and 1960s?

ANSWERS

# racism is the belief that some races are biologically superior to others

A1 believing that certain races are superior/inferior to others

A2 people of many different beliefs and cultures live alongside each other; some parts of the UK are more overtly multi-ethnic than others — London, Manchester, Leeds and Birmingham have sizeable ethnic populations, while rural areas are less ethnically diverse

A3 treating people less favourably on grounds of race or ethnic origin

A4 due to the break-up of the British empire and a shortage of labour in the UK workplace

*examiner's* note Racism and stirring up racial hatred are offences in the UK.

# Racial harmony

**Q1** What was made unlawful by the Race Relations Act?

**Q2** What does the Commission for Racial Equality do?

**Q3** Which UK public service body was declared to be 'institutionally racist' in the 1990s?

**Q4** Which church was partly responsible for the racist apartheid system in South Africa?

 ANSWERS

## people of different races living peacefully together

A1  racial discrimination in employment, housing, education and health

A2  it seeks to fight racism and give equal opportunities to all

A3  the police

A4  the Dutch Reformed church

***examiner's* note** Most churches work actively to promote racial equality and there are many anti-racist church programmes and opportunities for people from different racial backgrounds to participate in church. The congregations of many churches in major cities in the UK are predominantly non-white, while others have more culturally homogenous congregations, such as Korean or Portuguese.

# Racism and society today

**Q1** What is tokenism?

**Q2** What is positive discrimination?

**Q3** Why do some people disapprove of positive discrimination?

**Q4** Name one Church of England group concerned with combating racism.

ANSWERS

# the situation is better than in the past, but racism still exists

A1 including a minority figure (e.g. in a photograph) to ensure that a claim of racism cannot be made

A2 selecting someone for a job because of their colour (or sex), where minorities are under-represented

A3 it may lead to a better-qualified person not getting the job

A4 the Race and Community Relations Committee, the Committee on Black Anglican Concerns

***examiner's* note** Racism is not exclusively between blacks and whites. It can be between different racial groups of the same colour, such as Pakistani and Indian Asians.

# Martin Luther King, 1929–68

**Q1** What movement was led by Martin Luther King?

**Q2** What was King's great victory concerning transport?

**Q3** What award did King win in 1964?

**Q4** Who killed King?

**ANSWERS**

# US Baptist minister who fought for black civil rights

A1 the Civil Rights Movement in the USA

A2 an end to racial segregation on buses in the USA

A3 the Nobel Peace Prize

A4 James Earl Ray assassinated King in 1968

***examiner's* note** Martin Luther King gave a famous speech on 28 August 1963, including the well-known lines: 'I have a dream that my four little children will one day live in a nation where they will not be judged by the colour of their skin, but by the context of their character.'

# Religious pluralism

**Q1** What is a multi-faith society?

**Q2** Which non-Christian religion has the most followers in the UK?

**Q3** What is religious freedom?

ANSWERS

## the acceptance that all faiths have an equal right to exist and be practised

A1  one in which people of different religions live alongside each other

A2  Islam

A3  where members of all religions have the same freedom to worship

***examiner's* note** The lack of acceptance of other faiths is a cause of many problems in the world and has led to countless deaths in conflicts.

# Christianity and pluralism

**Q1** What is religious exclusivism?

**Q2** What is religious inclusivism?

**Q3** Why is pluralism a problem for some Christians?

**Q4** Name one organisation in the UK which seeks to heal divisions between faiths.

ANSWERS

A1 the belief that only one particular religion is true

A2 the belief that, while one religion is true, other faiths contain part of the truth

A3 many Christians believe that Christianity is the only valid route to salvation and a relationship with God

A4 the Council of Jews and Christians; the Inter-Faith Network for the UK

***examiner's* note** Some Christians may refer to John 14:6 to support the view that following Jesus is the only way to find God.

# Christianity and other faiths

**Q1** What is the name of the wars which Christians fought against Muslims for control of the Holy Land?

**Q2** What is an evangelist?

**Q3** What is a missionary?

**Q4** Why do some Christians believe it is important not to try to convert people of other faiths?

**ANSWERS** ▶▶

## many Christians consider it important to spread the gospel to people of other faiths

A1 the Crusades

A2 someone who teaches the gospel or Christian message to those who do not know it; literally, someone who spreads 'good news'

A3 someone who goes out into the world — overseas or in their own country — to work with people of other faiths and with people of no faith, and to support people in that community

A4 they believe that human beings have been given freedom to make their own decisions in all matters, including that of religion

***examiner's* note** In the UK, children of parents who do not share the Christian faith may legally not receive religious education or take part in worship in schools.

# Poverty

**Q1** Give three causes of poverty.

**Q2** What is meant by 'poverty of spirit'?

**Q3** What is relative poverty?

**Q4** What is absolute poverty?

ANSWERS ▶▶

# lack of sufficient means

A1 unemployment, homelessness, addiction, poor health, poor education

A2 a lack of self-respect and love

A3 where someone is considered to be poor in relation to another person in the same country

A4 where people lack the means necessary to provide for their basic needs

**examiner's note** The difference between 'relative' and 'absolute' poverty is that the former, in a country like the UK, might mean not owning a car, whereas the latter means not having enough money to buy food.

# Causes of world poverty

**Q1** Why is debt a problem in the poorest countries?

**Q2** What are cash crops?

**Q3** Why might the growing of cash crops lead to starvation?

**Q4** What is the cycle of poverty?

ANSWERS ▶▶

# the Brandt Report of 1980 revealed a significant imbalance between rich and poor nations

A1 repaying money owed in debts means that the poorest countries have little money left to buy food and essential services

A2 crops that can be sold quickly, e.g. tea, coffee, cotton

A3 cash crops are grown on land that could be used to grow food

A4 poor countries borrow money to buy food, then have to pay huge debts and cannot afford to provide the infrastructure necessary to get themselves out of poverty

***examiner's* note** In writing examination answers, don't assume that problems of world poverty can be solved simply. Try to look at a range of causes and possible solutions — not all problems are caused by the rich nations exploiting the poorer ones.

# Biblical teaching on poverty

**Q1** Name one parable of Jesus concerned with the relief of poverty.

**Q2** What is (i) almsgiving and (ii) tithing?

**Q3** What did Jesus ask the rich young man to do that he was unable to do (Mark 10:21)?

**Q4** Complete this famous biblical quotation: 'Blessed are the poor in spirit…'.

ANSWERS

poverty may bring people closer
to God, since they may feel they have
to depend on him for their needs

A1 the sheep and goats (Matthew 25:31–46); the rich fool
(Luke 12:13–21); the rich man and Lazarus (Luke 16:19–31)

A2 (i) giving money to the poor and needy
(ii) giving 10% of income to the church

A3 Jesus asked him to give all his wealth to the poor and then to
follow him

A4 '…for theirs is the kingdom of heaven.' (Matthew 5:3)

***examiner's* note** It is important to remember that being poor is not a
punishment from God and being wealthy is not a sin.

# Jesus' teachings on wealth and poverty

**Q1** What did Jesus teach in the parable of the rich fool (Luke 12:13–21)?

**Q2** What did Jesus teach in the story about the widow's offering (Mark 12:41–44)?

**Q3** Complete this famous biblical quotation: 'It is easier for a camel to go through the eye of a needle…'.

**Q4** What lesson about the use of money can be gained from the parable of the good Samaritan (Luke 10:25–37)?

ANSWERS

# Jesus condemned greed and the reckless use of money

A1 people should not store up treasure on earth, but instead should store up treasure in heaven

A2 although rich people gave more money than the widow, she gave all she had — this made her the most generous person

A3 '...than for a rich man to enter the kingdom of God.' (Mark 10:25)

A4 we should use our money generously and wisely to help others

**examiner's note** The teachings of Jesus should be used in answers to questions concerned with wealth and poverty. Quotations are especially useful.

# Christian Aid

**Q1** Which body established Christian Aid and when?

**Q2** What were its original aims and how does it help in times of disaster?

**Q3** How does Christian Aid raise money?

**Q4** What long-term aid is offered by Christian Aid?

ANSWERS ❯❯

# a religious relief organisation set up after the Second World War

A1 the British Council of Churches, in 1945

A2 to help homeless refugees and to fight worldwide poverty; by giving donations of food, medicine, blankets and shelter

A3 by voluntary donations and fundraising, particularly in the annual Christian Aid Week in May

A4 helping people to feed and provide for themselves

***examiner's* note** This is a Christian religious organisation. The ethos is based on its 'Prayer for a new Earth': '...a new Earth where the hungry will feast and the oppressed go free...'.

# CAFOD

**Q1** What does CAFOD stand for?

**Q2** Who set up CAFOD and when?

**Q3** How does CAFOD raise money?

**Q4** Give three examples of the ways CAFOD seeks to relieve poverty.

ANSWERS

# a Roman Catholic organisation for the relief of poverty

A1 Catholic Fund for Overseas Development

A2 Roman Catholic bishops in England and Wales in 1962

A3 through donations from the Catholic church, private individuals and agencies, government grants

A4 providing technology for long-term development, education, skills training and emergency aid

***examiner's* note** CAFOD's mission statement is: '…to promote human development and social justice in witness to the Christian faith and gospel values.'

# The Salvation Army

**Q1** Who founded the Salvation Army?

**Q2** How did it originally try to help the hungry and the homeless?

**Q3** How does it help alcoholics and drug addicts?

**Q4** What other work is done by the Salvation Army?

ANSWERS

founded in 1865 to relieve poverty, it is one of the main relief agencies working in the UK today

A1 William Booth

A2 by providing hot food in kitchens in poor and deprived areas and by providing hostels for the poor and shelters for single mothers

A3 by offering therapy and support in rehabilitation centres

A4 it helps locate missing persons; offers housing to the homeless and helps to rehabilitate them into society

***examiner's* note** The Salvation Army is a Christian religious organisation and not just a social welfare organisation, even though many of its activities overlap with those of the social services.

# Wealth

**Q1** Apart from money, what else can be a sign of wealth?

**Q2** Give two ways, other than by working, that people can accumulate wealth.

**Q3** What is the notion of 'fair wealth distribution'?

**Q4** 'According to the Bible, it is wrong to be wealthy.' True or false?

ANSWERS

A1 land, possessions

A2 inheritance, investments, gambling, business and property speculation

A3 wealth should be evenly spread among people

A4 false — wealth is not wrong; only misuse of it is wrong

***examiner's* note** One of the most famous biblical quotations about wealth is: 'You cannot serve both God and Money' (Matthew 6:24).

# Christian responses to wealth

**Q1** What do Christians believe is the moral duty of wealthy people?

**Q2** What does the Bible teach about God's judgement of the wealthy?

**Q3** What is a tithe?

**Q4** What is exploitation?

ANSWERS

# 'true happiness is not found in riches'
## (Catechism of the Catholic Church)

A1 to use their wealth to do good and to help the poor

A2 the wealthy will be judged according to their concern for the poor (Matthew 25:34–46)

A3 giving 10% of income to God's work

A4 accumulating wealth by taking unfair advantage of the poor and needy

**examiner's note** Christians should only obtain wealth in a lawful and moral way and must show compassion to others. The Bible teaches that Christians should set aside some of their money on a regular basis to help the poor.

# War and peace

**Q1** What is a 'Just War'?

**Q2** How did Jesus say that people should treat their enemies?

**Q3** Give three causes of war.

**Q4** What does the Roman Catholic church teach Christians about fighting in wars?

ANSWERS

# reasons why a Christian may go to war

A1 a war fought according to conditions of fairness and proportion — usually in self-defence or to help those being oppressed

A2 Jesus said 'love your enemies and pray for those who persecute you' (Matthew 5:44)

A3 human greed, selfishness, land, resources, wealth or national pride

A4 Christians should fight only as a 'last resort'

***examiner's* note** The 'Just War' is a set of guidelines laid down to help Christians to decide whether or not to fight in a war.

# Pacifism

**Q1** What is absolute pacifism?

**Q2** What is nuclear pacifism?

**Q3** What is a conscientious objector?

**Q4** When might a pacifist choose to fight?

ANSWERS

# the moral dilemma surrounding decisions to fight or not in a war

A1 where a person believes all fighting is wrong and will not fight in a war

A2 where a person will not fight in a nuclear war

A3 a pacifist who will not fight but may, for instance, join the armed forced as a doctor or nurse to help the wounded

A4 in self-defence, or against injustice and oppression

***examiner's note*** Not all pacifists refuse to fight in wars — many have fought in wars in the past, but only for a just cause.

# Punishment

**Q1** What is a crime?

**Q2** What is the purpose of punishment?

**Q3** Give three different examples of punishments given to criminals in the UK today.

**Q4** What does it mean to use punishment as a deterrent?

ANSWERS

A1 an act forbidden by the state and liable to punishment

A2 to make wrongdoers realise the wrong they have done and to try to ensure that they do not do it again

A3 imprisonment, fines and community service

A4 to put other people off doing a criminal act — often by showing how severe the punishment would be

***examiner's* note** Remember that punishment is often to do with keeping wrongdoers locked up so that they cannot hurt or threaten innocent people.

# Environmental issues (1)

**Q1** What is pollution?

**Q2** Identify four types of pollution.

**Q3** Why is waste such an important environmental issue today?

**Q4** What are non-renewable resources?

ANSWERS

# Christians believe that the world around us and its natural order are a gift from God

A1 the contamination of the environment

A2 land, air, water, and noise pollution

A3 most domestic waste cannot be recycled, and is not biodegradable (breaks down naturally if buried or exposed); it takes up space, spreads disease and releases dangerous chemicals into the environment

A4 resources that cannot be replaced once taken from the environment, including coal, gas, and oil

**examiner's note** The only way to decrease pollution is for all world nations to agree to limit it. Developed nations, such as the UK, have strict anti-pollution laws, but it is harder to enforce these on less developed countries, which still have to catch up in the race towards responsible industrialisation.

# Environmental issues (2)

**Q1** What is global warming?

**Q2** What effect does global warming have on the environment?

**Q3** What is deforestation?

**Q4** How can people help reduce global warming?

ANSWERS

## preserving the natural world for future generations is a responsibility that everyone should share

A1 the increase in the temperature of the earth's atmosphere, thought to be caused by the greenhouse effect

A2 sea levels rise, some areas have increased rain, others greater drought, extreme weather conditions increase, wildlife may be unable to adapt and will die out

A3 destruction of forested areas, leaving fewer trees to deal with increasing levels of carbon dioxide from burning fossil fuels

A4 reducing fuel consumption, recycling more and reducing use of cars

***examiner's* note** Carbon dioxide acts like the glass of a greenhouse, which allows the sun's energy in but does not allow it to get out. Thus the earth's temperature rises because trapped heat cannot escape, and the climate changes.

# Conservation

**Q1** What is stewardship?

**Q2** What responsibility were humans given at creation?

**Q3** In Christian belief, why does humanity struggle to fulfil this role?

**Q4** Why might some Christians have reservations about environmental conservation?

ANSWERS

# protecting, conserving and rebuilding the natural environment

A1   care for the environment and its resources

A2   to care for the earth and help it to yield the good harvests God designed it to produce

A3   after the Fall (see card 23) the task of farming and keeping the land became a struggle

A4   they fear it places too much emphasis on honouring the natural world, rather than tending to the needs of humankind

***examiner's* note** Failure to conserve the planet is not compatible with showing love to your neighbour, both in the present and future generations

# Vegetarianism

**Q1** What is vegetarian food?

**Q2** What is vegan food?

**Q3** What moral reasons may be offered for vegetarianism?

**Q4** How might Christians support vegetarianism?

ANSWERS ))

# adopting a meat-free diet

A1 food prepared without using primary meat products: the flesh, muscle, blood, bones or internal organs

A2 food prepared without making use of primary or secondary meat products, including eggs and dairy products

A3 it does not condone or contribute to causing pain and suffering to animals; the human diet should not be based on dead products

A4 God did not give humans meat to eat until after the flood (Genesis 9)

***examiner's note*** Some Christians are opposed to vegetarianism on the grounds that Jesus permitted his disciples to eat all foods.